# YLE Tests
# Flyers

*Four tests for Cambridge English: Flyers*

PETRINA CLIFF

**OXFORD**

UNIVERSITY PRESS

# OXFORD
UNIVERSITY PRESS

Great Clarendon Street, Oxford OX2 6DP

Oxford University Press is a department of the University of Oxford.
It furthers the University's objective of excellence in research, scholarship,
and education by publishing worldwide in

Oxford  New York

Auckland  Cape Town  Dar es Salaam  Hong Kong  Karachi
Kuala Lumpur  Madrid  Melbourne  Mexico City  Nairobi
New Delhi  Shanghai  Taipei  Toronto

With offices in

Argentina  Austria  Brazil  Chile  Czech Republic  France  Greece
Guatemala  Hungary  Italy  Japan  Poland  Portugal  Singapore
South Korea  Switzerland  Thailand  Turkey  Ukraine  Vietnam

OXFORD and OXFORD ENGLISH are registered trade marks of
Oxford University Press in the UK and in certain other countries

ISBN: 978 0 19 457720 5

Printed in China

This book is printed on paper from certified and well-managed sources.

ACKNOWLEDGEMENTS

*Commissioned illustrations by*: John Haslem pp.4,8, 9, 10, 12,14, 15, 16, 23, 25, 26,
30, 31, 32, 34, 36, 37, 38, 45, 47, 48, 52, 53, 54, 56, 58, 59, 60, 67, 69, 70, 74, 75,
76, 78, 80, 81, 82, 89, 91; Mark Ruffle pp.6,7, 18, 20, 22, 24, 28, 29, 40, 42, 44,
46, 50, 51, 62, 64, 66, 68, 72, 73, 84, 86, 88, 90.

# Contents

# Part 1

– 5 questions –

**Listen and draw lines. There is one example.**

David        Bill        Jane        Jill

Sam                Betty                Paul

# Part 2

**Listen and write. There is one example.**

<table>
<tr><td></td><td>Address:</td><td>25 ____Hillman____ Road<br>Frenchly</td></tr>
<tr><td>1</td><td>Full Name:</td><td>_____ Taylor</td></tr>
<tr><td>2</td><td>Age:</td><td>_____</td></tr>
<tr><td>3</td><td>Problem:</td><td>_____ and a _____</td></tr>
<tr><td>4</td><td>See Doctor:</td><td>_____ afternoon</td></tr>
<tr><td>5</td><td>What time?</td><td>_____</td></tr>
</table>

# Part 3

**What are William's friends doing in the school holidays?**

**Listen and write a letter in each box. There is one example.**

Robert [B]

David [ ]

Betty [ ]

Richard [ ]

Helen [ ]

Sarah [ ]

**A**

**B**

**C**

**D**

**E**

**F**

**G**

**H**

# Part 4

– 5 questions –

**Listen and tick (✔) the box. There is one example.**

Who is Michael's art teacher?

A ✔     B ☐     C ☐

1   Where's the art room at school?

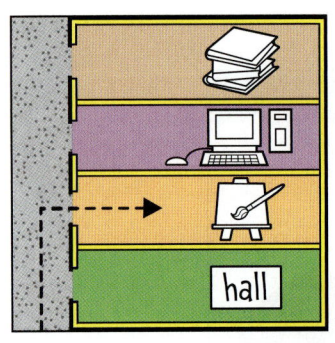 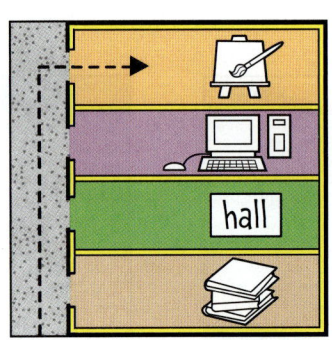 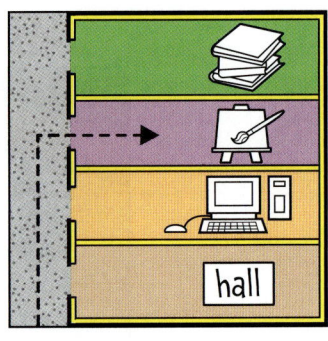

A ☐     B ☐     C ☐

2   What time does the club finish?

A ☐     B ☐     C ☐

3   What's Michael going to make at art club?

A ☐

B ☐

C ☐

4   What's Michael going to use to make his toy?

A ☐

B ☐

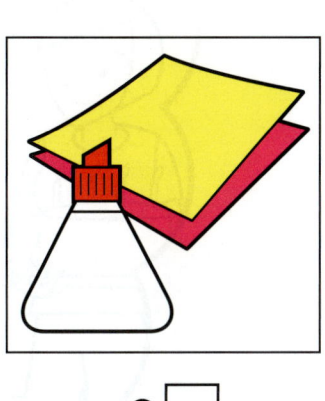

C ☐

5   Who is Michael making the toy for?

A ☐

B ☐

C ☐

# Part 5

## Listen and colour and write and draw. There is one example.

# Reading & Writing

## Part I

– 10 questions –

**Look and read. Choose the correct words and write them on the lines. There is one example.**

a museum          soap          sugar          a comic          a post office

artists

a hotel

a drum

actors

astronauts

a torch

flour

a swing

a tent

a chemist's

| | | |
|---|---|---|
| People stay here when they're on holiday. | | _a hotel_ |
| 1 | This can be brown or white and you use it when you're making bread or pasta. | _____ |
| 2 | Children like to play on this in the park or in the garden. | _____ |
| 3 | These are people who work in the theatre or on TV. | _____ |
| 4 | Children love playing with this. They hit it and it makes a lot of noise. | _____ |
| 5 | You use this to get clean when you have a bath or a shower. | _____ |
| 6 | Chocolates and sweets are made with this. It tastes good but it can give you toothache. | _____ |
| 7 | People sleep in this when they go camping by the sea or in the countryside. | _____ |
| 8 | When you feel ill you can go here to buy some medicine. | _____ |
| 9 | These people need to be very good at drawing and painting pictures. | _____ |
| 10 | You can use this when you go outside at night and you want to see. | _____ |

# Part 2

**Look and read. Write yes or no.**

**Examples**

There's a suitcase and a boat on top of the car.     _____yes_____

The driver of the car is looking at one of the boys.     _____no_____

**Questions**

1  There are some flowers in an upstairs window.  _____

2  The guitar is behind the rucksack.  _____

3  A man is sitting in the garden and reading
   a book.  _____

4  The boy who's wearing shorts and a white
   T-shirt has fallen into a suitcase.  _____

5  On the balcony of the house on the left,
   there's a boy who's waving.  _____

6  The scarf next to the boy carrying a square
   suitcase has got spots on it.  _____

7  The woman who's standing with her hands on
   the wall is laughing.  _____

# Part 3

Sally is talking to her friend, Vicky. What does Vicky say?

Read the conversation and choose the best answer. Write a letter (A–H) for each answer.

You do not need to use all the letters. There is one example.

**Example**

> **Sally:** So where have you been?
>
> **Vicky:** _____F_____

**Questions**

1 **Sally:** Did you buy anything nice?

 **Vicky:** _____

2 **Sally:** Let's see them then.

 **Vicky:** _____

3 **Sally:** They're lovely! Where did you get them?

 **Vicky:** _____

4 **Sally:** Oh, I'd like to go there!

 **Vicky:** _____

5 **Sally:** That'd be great, but do you want to go again so soon?

 **Vicky:** _____

A  Do you like them?

B  Oh, I don't mind. Let's do it!

C  From a little shop next to the bank.

D  Well, I got a handbag from that shop you like.

E  Yes, I think you would!

F  Oh, just shopping in town.    **(Example)**

G  Only a pair of jeans and a T-shirt.

H  Well, what about tomorrow then?

# Part 4

**Read the story. Choose a word from the box. Write the correct word next to numbers 1–5. There is one example.**

My name's David. One day I was walking home when I saw a
_____fire_____ in the downstairs window of a very big house. I went
to the **(1)** _____ door and shouted loudly but nobody came.
There was a telephone in the street near the house so I phoned and
told someone about the fire. After about five minutes a fire engine
with blue lights on the top came round the **(2)** _____ . It
was very exciting! Firemen were running everywhere, throwing
water on the fire and then, suddenly, everything was all right again.

I went into the house with the firemen. The kitchen was badly burnt
and it **(3)** _____ terrible but the other rooms in the house
were fine. Then this man arrived. I knew him! He was a famous
footballer but he was also the man who lived in the big house. He
**(4)** _____ me very much and asked me for my name and
address. Then, two days later, a letter arrived for me. Inside the
**(5)** _____ there were two tickets to see my favourite team
play! How good was that?

(6) **Now choose the best name for the story.**

**Tick one box.**

David and the big surprise ☐

David and the empty house ☐

David and the fireman ☐

# Part 5

**Look at the picture and read the story. Write some words to complete the sentences about the story. You can use 1, 2, 3 or 4 words.**

## The painter

My name's Bill and I'm a painter. It can be a difficult job when the weather's bad but I still like it. Well, yesterday I went to paint a house for a woman called Mrs Hill but when I got to the house there was no-one in. I decided to start painting because it was a big house and I had just two days to finish it.

At about midday I stopped for lunch and went to a cafe round the corner. I asked for burger and chips. That's my favourite meal. But there were no burgers so I had fish and chips instead. Well, I was eating my food when a woman phoned me. She said, 'Where are you?' and I answered, 'I'm having my lunch!' I was surprised because she was very unfriendly and she didn't say she liked my painting.

At two o'clock I went back to the house but there was still no-one there! Then I saw a woman in the garden of the house next door. She looked very angry so I said 'What's the matter?'. Her answer made me feel terrible. She said 'I'm waiting for a man to paint my house. He said he'd come this morning but he hasn't arrived yet.' 'What's your name?' I asked her. 'Mrs Hill' she said! I was painting the wrong house! I picked up my paint and brushes and ran away!

## Examples

Bill's job is sometimes ___difficult_____ if the weather isn't nice.

Yesterday Bill was going ___to paint_____ Mrs Hill's house.

## Questions

I  When Bill arrived at the house there _____ at home.

2  Bill wanted to start work because there were only _____ to do the job.

3  Bill ate _____ for lunch.

4  Bill thought the woman sounded _____ on the telephone.

5  Bill felt _____ when the woman in the garden answered his question.

6  The woman was waiting for someone to _____.

7  Bill suddenly understood that he was painting _____.

# Part 6

– 10 questions –

## Read the text. Choose the right words and write them on the lines.

### What can robots do?

**Example**

Robots ____aren't____ just children's toys. Robots can

1 do many things to help us with _____ work.
They do all kinds of boring jobs. In some factories,
for example, they can put sweets carefully into

2 boxes and in _____ factories they make cars
with no help at all!

3 We also use robots _____ help us understand
4 more about science. Robots _____ been
to the moon to get rocks for us to study and they
5 also visit other planets _____ people can't go.

An 'android' is a robot which looks like a person.
6 'Asimo' is the name _____ one 'android'
robot. It can't feel happy or sad, of course,
7 _____ it can walk, sit down and stand up. It
climbs up and down stairs too. But can it think? Well,
8 yes, but only _____ other people give it
information first. It can't cook and clean or
9 _____ your homework for you. Not yet! But
10 one day that _____ happen!

| **Example** | don't | isn't | aren't |
| 1 | his | our | their |
| 2 | other | much | every |
| 3 | to | for | by |
| 4 | has | have | having |
| 5 | what | why | where |
| 6 | of | on | at |
| 7 | so | but | or |
| 8 | if | so | then |
| 9 | do | doing | did |
| 10 | might | won't | shall |

# Part 7

**Read the diary and write the missing words. Write one word on each line.**

## Thursday 22ⁿᵈ June

**Example**

Today was a horrible day! _____This_____ morning I

1  went to the dentist and he _____ at my
teeth. He wasn't very happy with them! Then I was
late for school and I had a maths test. It was very

2  hard and I couldn't _____ it at all!
And then, this evening, I wanted to go to the cinema

3  to see a film _____ my friends. But Mum said

4  I _____ to stay at home and finish my

5  homework. It's only half _____ nine and I'm
so bored. I hope tomorrow is better!

Sarah

# Speaking

## Find the Differences

23

# Information Exchange

## Candidate's copy

| Emma's DVD | |
|---|---|
| Name | Space story |
| Who / gave | aunt |
| What / about | two astronauts |
| When / watch | yesterday |
| Exciting / boring | boring |

| William's DVD | |
|---|---|
| Name | ? |
| Who / gave | ? |
| What / about | ? |
| When / watch | ? |
| Exciting / boring | ? |

## Examiner's copy

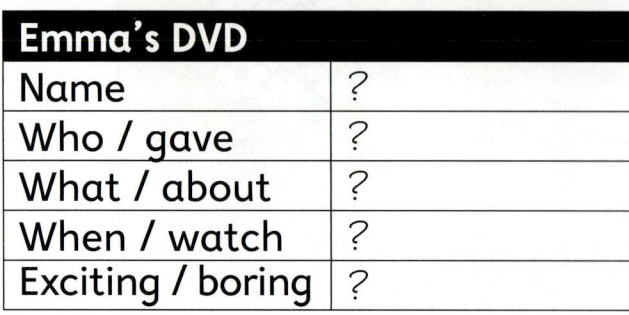

| Emma's DVD | |
|---|---|
| Name | ? |
| Who / gave | ? |
| What / about | ? |
| When / watch | ? |
| Exciting / boring | ? |

| William's DVD | |
|---|---|
| Name | Island Adventure |
| Who / gave | uncle |
| What / about | three pirates |
| When / watch | last week |
| Exciting / boring | exciting |

**Picture Story**

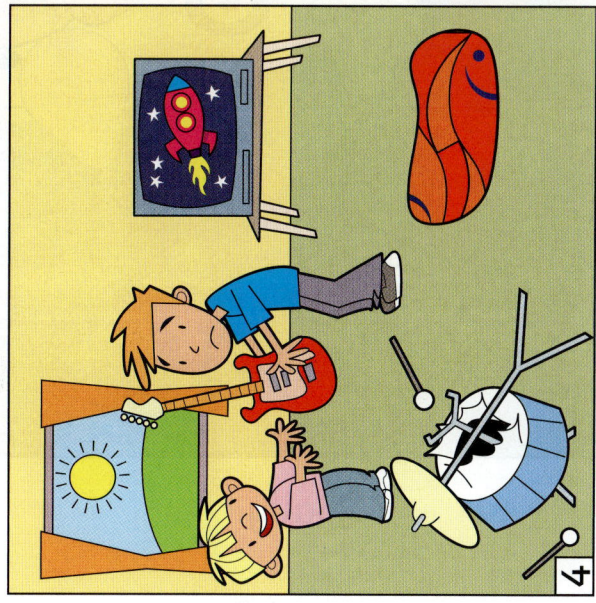

25

# Part I
## – 5 questions –

**Listen and draw lines. There is one example.**

Fred            Lucy            William          Robert

Sally                    Katy                    Paul

# Part 2

– 5 questions –

**Listen and write. There is one example.**

## HISTORY HOMEWORK

Talk to an old person you know. Find out the answers.

Age: _____86_____

1 Name: _____ Smith (my grandfather)

2 Lived where? in a _____ in north London (only two bedrooms)

3 Family: five _____ and parents

4 First job: _____

5 Hobbies: driving expensive cars
looking at _____ _____

# Part 3

**Where did Mrs Black take these pictures?**

**Listen and write a letter in each box. There is one example.**

Aunt Pat ☐ E

Uncle Fred ☐

Dad ☐

Alex ☐

Sue ☐

Mum ☐

A

B

C

D

E

F

G

H

# Part 4

– 5 questions –

**Listen and tick (✔) the box. There is one example.**

What's Jane going to study next year?

A ☐

B ✔

C ☐

1   Which is Jane's room?

A ☐

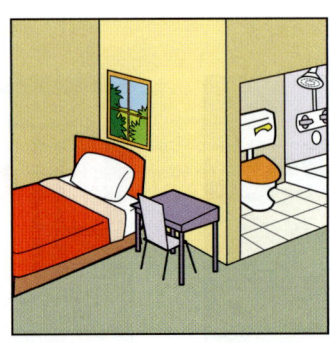

B ☐

C ☐

2   Which girl has Jane already met?

A ☐

B ☐

C ☐

3   Which suitcase is Jane going to take?

A ☐

B ☐

C ☐

4   When is Jane going to college?

A ☐

B ☐

C ☐

5   What's Jane going to do this evening?

A ☐

B ☐

C ☐

# Part 5

– 5 questions –

## Listen and colour and write and draw. There is one example.

# Reading & Writing

## Part 1

– 10 questions –

**Look and read. Choose the correct words and write them on the lines.
There is one example.**

octopuses      meetings      a scarf      dinosaurs      a journalist

news

offices

plastic

a comb

| | |
|---|---|
| You should go and see this person if you have toothache. | _a dentist_ |
| 1  Some animals have this because they need to be warm in the winter. | _____ |
| 2  Businessmen and businesswomen work at their desks in these rooms. | _____ |
| 3  You can use this when you want to make your hair look tidy. | _____ |
| 4  These animals live in the sea and they have eight legs. | _____ |
| 5  These animals lived on our planet a long time ago and are now extinct. | _____ |
| 6  You wear these on your hands in winter when it's cold. | _____ |
| 7  A bird uses these when it wants to fly. | _____ |
| 8  When you go shopping, the bags you often get in supermarkets are made of this. | _____ |
| 9  Women often wear these on their legs when they're wearing skirts or dresses. | _____ |
| 10  This person writes in a newspaper about things that have happened in the world. | _____ |

tights

wings

gloves

fur

a secretary      a dentist

# Part 2

**Look and read. Write yes or no.**

**Examples**

| | |
|---|---|
| The time on the clock says five o'clock. | _yes_ |
| The baby in the car is sleeping. | _no_ |

## Questions

1   The man who's wearing a green shirt is also
    wearing a belt.                                    _____

2   A boy with curly hair is throwing a torch into
    the bin.                                           _____

3   There's a picture of a taxi on the wall above
    the door.                                          _____

4   The mechanic who's standing under the blue
    car is very dirty.                                 _____

5   There's a radio behind the child who's holding
    a small car.                                       _____

6   Outside in the road there's a girl posting a
    letter.                                            _____

7   The woman with a bag is wearing a skirt.           _____

# Part 3

Jack is talking to his teacher, Mrs White. What does Mrs White say?

Read the conversation and choose the best answer. Write a letter (A–H) for each answer.

You do not need to use all the letters. There is one example.

**Example**

| | | |
|---|---|---|
| Jack: | Hello Mrs White! | |
| Mrs White: | _____ D _____ | |

**Questions**

1  Jack:  Oh, I'm really sorry but I couldn't do it at the weekend! I was ill you see

Mrs White: _____

2  Jack:  I know, and I'll do it tonight, Mrs White, I promise!

Mrs White: _____

3  Jack:  Oh yes, I thought that was very difficult!

Mrs White: _____

4  Jack:  Oh, but I've got a football match, Mrs White!

Mrs White: _____

5  Jack:  Could I do it later perhaps?

Mrs White: _____

A  I'm sorry but, you can't, Jack!

B  You'll have to miss that.

C  Yes, well, I'm sorry but I want you to do it again this lunch time.

D  Oh, Jack! Can I have a word about your homework please?          **(Example)**

E  OK Jack. But I also want to talk about the English test you did yesterday!

F  But it's Thursday now Jack!

G  Oh, I hope you're feeling better.

H  Yes, well you won't forget this time, will you?

# Part 4

**Read the story. Choose a word from the box. Write the correct word next to numbers 1–5. There is one example.**

One evening in ___summer___ I was climbing in the mountains with my older brother, Robert. After about an hour, Robert looked at the map but he couldn't (1) _____ out where we were. There was a castle in front of us but it wasn't on the map. We walked up to the big door together. Suddenly an ugly old woman was standing there! She was wearing a (2) _____ black dress.

We went inside. It was very dark in the castle and we were both afraid. The old woman didn't say anything but started to walk away from us. My brother (3) _____ 'Don't go with her!' but I didn't listen. I (4) _____ her up some stairs. At the top there was another smaller door. The woman opened it and there, in front of me, was a room (5) _____ of sweets! I went inside and the door closed behind me. It wouldn't open again.

And then I heard someone in the room. It was my brother. 'Come on Harry! Wake up, you'll be late for school!' he said.

(6) Now choose the best name for the story.

**Tick one box.**

The bad dream          ☐

The famous castle      ☐

The poor woman         ☐

# Part 5

**Look at the picture and read the story. Write some words to complete the sentences about the story. You can use 1, 2, 3 or 4 words.**

## Trip to the museum

My name's Harry. Last week my teacher took our class to The Museum of History in the city. We went by bus because it was cheaper than the train. Before we went inside, the teacher gave us a map of the museum and said 'It's half past nine now. You're free to look round but you must meet me here at half past eleven. Don't be late!' I didn't have a watch but my friend, Sam, did. We walked in!

There were clothes and things people used in the old days everywhere. It was very interesting. You could read people's old diaries too. But Sam said they were boring. He looked at his map and saw there were some pyramids in the basement so we went to find them. They were great! Then we went into the museum shop to buy some things. There were pens, pencils, and books about the museum. We couldn't decide what to buy! In the end I bought a ruler for my brother and Sam got a fan with a picture of the museum on it for his little sister.

Then Sam looked at his watch. We were very late! We ran up the stairs to the front of the museum and looked for our teacher. He wasn't there. Suddenly a bus went past. All our friends from class were looking through the window and laughing and waving at us. But our teacher wasn't laughing!

**Examples**

Harry went with his teacher and the class to a place in
___the city_____ called The Museum of History.

The bus _____was cheaper than_____ the train so they all went by
bus.

**Questions**

1   The teacher told the children to come back again at
_____.

2   Sam said that the _____ were boring.

3   The boys went to _____ to find some
pyramids.

4   Next the boys decided to _____ from the
museum shop.

5   Sam bought a fan for _____.

6   The boys went to the front of the museum but their teacher
_____.

7   The boys saw that their _____ were
already on the bus!

# Part 6

**Read the text. Choose the right words and write them on the lines.**

## Come to London

| Example | There are many famous places __to__ visit in |
| --- | --- |
| | London. The most famous, perhaps, is 'Buckingham |
| 1 | Palace' _____ it's the Queen's home. 'Tower |
| 2 | Bridge' is over 100 years old and you _____ |
| | see it from one of the boats on the 'River Thames'. |

| 3 | London _____ lots of things for families to |
| --- | --- |
| 4 | do together. _____ you want to go |
| | shopping, Harrods is London's most famous store |
| | but it's very expensive. You'll find that markets sell |
| 5 | some very nice things and are _____ |
| 6 | cheaper. And you must visit 'Hamleys' _____ |
| | is London's best toy shop. |

| | What about food? There are many restaurants |
| --- | --- |
| 7 | in London _____ the 'Rainforest Café' is |
| | very good for children. When you go inside you |
| 8 | _____ see paintings of jungle animals |
| | everywhere! And in summer it's nice to have |
| 9 | _____ picnic in one of London's lovely, |
| | green parks. When it's rainy, go to the cinema at |
| 10 | the science museum and _____ a rocket go |
| | up into space! London's a great place for a holiday! |

| **Example** | to | for | by |
|---|---|---|---|
| 1 | when | because | while |
| 2 | can | like | want |
| | | | |
| 3 | is | has | gives |
| 4 | Before | Then | If |
| | | | |
| 5 | very | much | most |
| 6 | what | that | which |
| | | | |
| 7 | but | so | or |
| 8 | have | would | will |
| 9 | a | an | the |
| 10 | watching | watch | watched |

# Part 7

**Read the diary and write the missing words. Write one word on each line.**

|  | Dear Sue, |
|---|---|
| **Example** | I'm just writing because I want ___*to*___ say |
| 1 | well done in your piano exam. I can't _____ |
|  | the piano at all. You're so clever! I shall listen to you |
| 2 | _____ I come to visit you in the summer. |
| 3 | _____ is your brother now? I hope he's |
| 4 | feeling much _____. Your mum told me he's |
|  | had a very bad cold. |
| 5 | The weather here is lovely! And it's _____ |
|  | long until the holidays now. See you all then. |
|  | I can't wait! |
|  | Love, |
|  | Grandma |

# Speaking

**Find the Differences**

45

## Information Exchange

### Candidate's copy

| David's holiday | |
| --- | --- |
| Where | mountains |
| Weather good | no – windy |
| How long | ten days |
| What / do | cycling |
| Who / with | school friends |

| Helen's holiday | |
| --- | --- |
| Where | ? |
| Weather good | ? |
| How long | ? |
| What / do | ? |
| Who / with | ? |

### Examiner's copy

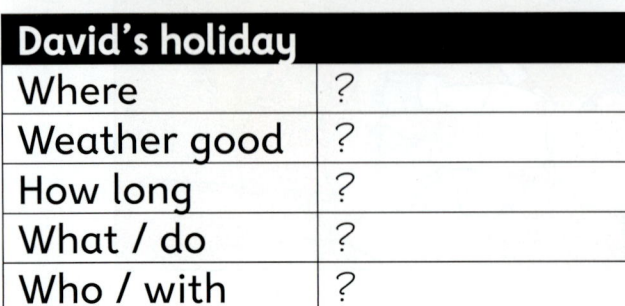

| David's holiday | |
| --- | --- |
| Where | ? |
| Weather good | ? |
| How long | ? |
| What / do | ? |
| Who / with | ? |

| Helen's holiday | |
| --- | --- |
| Where | sea |
| Weather good | yes – sunny |
| How long | two weeks |
| What / do | swimming |
| Who / with | family |

# Picture Story

# Test 3   Listening

## Part 1
– 5 questions –

**Listen and draw lines. There is one example.**

Mary          John          Peter          Helen

Michael          Sarah          Richard

# Part 2

**Listen and write. There is one example.**

| | Name: | _____Cynthia_____ Jones |
|---|---|---|
| 1 | Address: | 33 _____ Road Castletown |
| | Done shop work before? | yes |
| 2 | When? | last _____ (for three weeks) |
| 3 | Wants job because? | she wants _____ for a holiday. |
| 4 | Can work which days? | _____ only |
| 5 | Hours wanted? | from _____ to 5 p.m. |

# Part 3

– 5 questions –

**Where did Mrs Banks buy the things for the party?**

**Listen and write a letter in each box. There is one example.**

| | | |
|---|---|---|
| | shoes | D |
| | CDs | |
| | pizzas | |
| | sweets | |
| | cake | |
| | diaries | |

A

B

C

D

E

F

G

H

# Part 4

– 5 questions –

**Listen and tick (✔) the box. There is one example.**

What time did Richard see the doctor?

A ☐          B ✔          C ☐

1   What did the doctor tell Richard to do?

A ☐          B ☐          C ☐

2   What's the matter with Richard now?

A ☐          B ☐          C ☐

3   What does Richard ask his mother for?

A ☐

B ☐

C ☐

4   What homework has Richard got to do?

A ☐

B ☐

C ☐

5   When is Richard going to go back to school?

A ☐

B ☐

C ☐

# Part 5

*– 5 questions –*

## Listen and colour and write and draw. There is one example.

Can anyone
work _____
tonight?

# Reading & Writing

## Part 1

**Look and read. Choose the correct words and write them on the lines.**
**There is one example.**

a husband     autumn     scissors     shelves     midnight

You ride on this in a park or on the road.
You need to work hard when you go up hills. _a bicycle_

bins

1  This is the name for a man who is
   married to a woman. _____

2  You throw paper and other things in
   these when you don't want them. _____

3  This is often blue in the day and at night
   you can see the moon and stars here. _____

pockets

4  This person works outside in the fields
   and often has lots of animals. _____

5  These are often made of wood and you
   put books, photographs and other
   things on them. _____

6  This is a time of the year and it comes
   between summer and winter. _____

sky

7  You can't see this but animals and plants
   need it to live, and we do too. _____

8  This person works in a hospital and wears
   a uniform. _____

a wife

9  Coats and trousers often have these and
   you can put things in them. _____

10 This time of day is very late. It usually
   comes after you've gone to bed. _____

midday

spring

a nurse

air

a farmer           a bicycle

# Part 2

– 7 questions –

**Look and read. Write yes or no.**

**Examples**

The man who's wearing a uniform looks very angry. _____yes_____

There's a chair above a picture of some spiders. _____no_____

## Questions

1   The woman who's looking at the yellow camel is wearing a hat.   _____

2   There's a boy holding one of the dinosaur's legs.   _____

3   The baby who's sleeping has dropped some sweets.   _____

4   One of the woman's gloves is lying on the floor behind her.   _____

5   There's an umbrella under the chair which is on the right of the picture.   _____

6   A boy is sitting next to the snake's head and he's eating a sandwich.   _____

7   There are some butterflies above the girl with the camera and they've got spots on them.   _____

# Part 3

– 5 questions –

Richard is talking to his friend, Paul. What does Paul say?

Read the conversation and choose the best answer. Write a letter (A–H) for each answer.

You do not need to use all the letters. There is one example.

**Example**

| | | |
|---|---|---|
| Richard: | I'm going on holiday tomorrow. |
| Paul: | _____F_____ |

**Questions**

1  Richard: I'm going skiing in the mountains!

   Paul: _____

2  Richard: My best friend and his family.

   Paul: _____

3  Richard: Once, but that was years ago.

   Paul: _____

4  Richard: I'm not sure but I'll soon find out!

   Paul: _____

5  Richard: Thanks. Are you doing anything nice?

   Paul: _____

A   Just staying at home with my family, but it'll be OK.

B   Well I hope you have a great time!

C   That sounds a bit dangerous! Why?

D   I think I'd like that!

E   Great! And have you ever been before?

F   You must be excited! Where are you going?                    **(Example)**

G   That sounds fun. Who with?

H   Do you think you'll remember how to do it?

# Part 4

– 6 questions –

**Read the story. Choose a word from the box. Write the correct word next to numbers 1–5. There is one example.**

Today was a terrible day! It all started this morning. It was
___time___ to go to school but my brother Sam wasn't ready. He couldn't find his English **(1)** _____. We looked for ages then I found it under the sofa. And then Mum said she hadn't got her car keys. We looked for them but we couldn't find them anywhere. We have to be at school at nine o'clock and it was already half past eight. The school isn't near our house but we **(2)** _____ to walk there.

At lunchtime all my friends went outside to play games but I had to **(3)** _____ in class and do my Maths. It was horrible! At the end of the day, Mum came to get us and we walked back home again. When we got home we were very **(4)** _____. Then, suddenly, Sam said 'Look!' and pointed to the car. There, in the car door, were the keys! We all **(5)** _____ until Mum said quietly, 'I can't find the keys to the house now!'

(6) Now choose the best name for the story.

**Tick one box.**

Mum's lost keys ☐

My interesting day ☐

Sam gets it wrong ☐

# Part 5

**Look at the picture and read the story. Write some words to complete the sentences about the story. You can use 1, 2, 3 or 4 words.**

## Going to the airport

My name's Nick. Last summer I went on holiday with my sister, Kim, and my parents. We got up early in the morning because we were going by plane. We packed our suitcases the night before. When Dad woke me up I was very tired, and I didn't eat any breakfast because I wasn't hungry.

Then we all got in the car and dad started to drive to the airport. It was very foggy and we couldn't see the road at all. Suddenly, there was a loud noise as Dad hit the car in front of us. We weren't going fast so it wasn't a bad accident but the man in the other car was very angry and shouted at Dad. I was scared and my sister started crying. The man asked for our address and Dad wrote it down for him on some paper. Then Dad started driving again, very slowly this time.

When we got to the airport we were late and Mum said 'We've missed the plane now!' She was very angry too. Poor Dad! But when we got inside the airport Mum found that our plane was still there. She was happier then. So we went to the airport café and waited to go on our holiday. And it was the best holiday ever!

## Examples

Nick's sister is called _____Kim_____

The family _____got up early_____ that morning to go on holiday.

## Questions

1  That morning Nick had no breakfast because he
   _____.

2  In the car, it was very difficult to see the road because it was
   _____.

3  Nick heard a _____ when his dad had the accident.

4  Nick felt _____ when the man shouted at his dad.

5  Nick's dad _____ his address and gave it to the man.

6  After the accident, Nick's dad decided that he should drive to the airport _____.

7  Nick's mum was happy when she heard that the plane
   _____.

# Part 6

– 10 questions –

**Read the text. Choose the right words and write them on the lines.**

## What do journalists do?

**Example**    Journalists do _____*many*_____ different things at
             work. Here is an idea of some of the things

1            journalists do each day. Before they _____
             write anything, journalists must leave the office and

2            ask people lots of questions _____ they
             need to find out information for their stories first.

3            They often take a tape recorder with _____
             so they don't forget the information they've
             heard. Then they go back to their office and write

4            their stories very _____ on the computer.
             News stories are often short and give the

5            _____ important information about

6            things that _____ just happened. They often

7            work with photographers _____ take
             pictures which help to tell the stories.

             When they have written their stories, journalists

8            check that they haven't made _____
             mistakes at all. They must be sure that

9            _____ is correct before the stories go
             into the newspaper. It isn't easy to be a journalist

10           but it's _____ boring!

64

| **Example** | other | more | many |
|---|---|---|---|
| 1 | shall | can | could |
| 2 | but | when | because |
| 3 | it | him | them |
| 4 | quick | quicker | quickly |
| 5 | best | most | much |
| 6 | are | has | have |
| 7 | who | how | what |
| 8 | any | some | lots |
| 9 | something | everything | nothing |
| 10 | always | often | never |

# Part 7

**Read the diary and write the missing words. Write one word on each line.**

Dear Emma,

**Example** I can't wait _____until_____ you come and see me

1 next week. We'll _____ a great time

together. I know you're coming by plane so I'll

2 meet you _____ the airport with my family.

3 There are _____ of different things to do

here so I know you won't be bored. On your first

4 day we're _____ to go into town to do some

5 shopping. The _____ is very rainy here in

February so bring your umbrella!

See you very soon.

Lots of love,

Sarah

# Speaking

## Find the Differences

Examiner's copy

Candidate's copy

# Information Exchange

## Candidate's copy

| Robert's restaurant | |
| --- | --- |
| Where | opposite / police station |
| Who / with | parents |
| Time | 7.30 |
| How / go | car |
| What / eat | chicken / chips |

| Sarah's restaurant | |
| --- | --- |
| Where | ? |
| Who / with | ? |
| Time | ? |
| How / go | ? |
| What / eat | ? |

## Examiner's copy

| Robert's restaurant | |
| --- | --- |
| Where | ? |
| Who / with | ? |
| Time | ? |
| How / go | ? |
| What / eat | ? |

| Sarah's restaurant | |
| --- | --- |
| Where | next / fire station |
| Who / with | friends |
| Time | 8.30 |
| How / go | bus |
| What / eat | burger / salad |

# Picture Story

69

# Part I
– 5 questions –

**Listen and draw lines. There is one example.**

Emma      Alex      Jack      Vicky

Anna            Jim            Harry

# Part 2

**Listen and write. There is one example.**

| | | |
|---|---|---|
| Name: | Bethany _Phillips_ | |
| 1 | Address: | 27 _____ Street |
| | | Brighton |
| 2 | What lost? | a _____ handbag |
| 3 | Where lost? | at the _____ |
| 4 | Anything inside? | money, a _____ and two _____ |
| 5 | Phone number: | _____ |

71

# Part 3

**Where are the things that Jill has left at her Aunt's house?**

**Listen and write a letter in each box. There is one example.**

| | | |
|---|---|---|
| | brush | [C] |
| | key | [ ] |
| | umbrella | [ ] |
| | belt | [ ] |
| | torch | [ ] |
| | comb | [ ] |

**A**

**B**

**C**

**D**

**E**

**F**

**G**

**H**

# Part 4

– 5 questions –

**Listen and tick (✔) the box. There is one example.**

Where's William going to go with his school friends?

A ☐

B ☐

C ✔

1   What has William forgotten to put in his rucksack?

A ☐

B ☐

C ☐

2   What's the weather going to be like?

A ☐

B ☐

C ☐

3    Where's William going to stay?

A ☐                B ☐                C ☐

4    How's William going to get there?

A ☐                B ☐                C ☐

5    What doesn't William want to eat when he's away?

   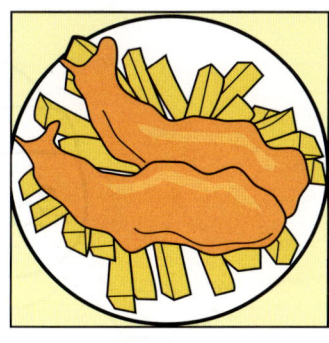   

A ☐                B ☐                C ☐

# Part 5

## Listen and colour and write and draw. There is one example.

Café

HOT _____

# Reading & Writing

## Part I

– 10 questions –

**Look and read. Choose the correct words and write them on the lines. There is one example.**

a player      traffic      deserts      bridges      a rocket

castles

wool

a team

metal

You can go here for help if someone steals your money.     _police station_

1  This is a group of people who play a sport together, for example, football.    _____

2  This is very noisy and you find a lot of it on the road when people are going to work or coming home again.    _____

3  This comes from sheep and we make clothes and blankets with it.    _____

4  In this competition everyone runs together and the person who comes first wins.    _____

5  This comes from trees and people make tables, chairs and other things with it.    _____

6  These are smaller than mountains and you climb them when you go to the countryside.    _____

7  This is like a plane but it goes into space.   _____

8  You walk over these when you want to go across roads or rivers.    _____

9  You can see through this and bottles are sometimes made of it.    _____

10  In children's books, a queen might live in one of these.    _____

a race

hills

glass

wood

police station      a fire engine

# Part 2

– 7 questions –

## Look and read. Write **yes** or **no**.

**Examples**

There are two clouds on the left of the picture. _____ yes

The father of the two children is wearing a coat. _____ no

**Questions**

1   Both doors of the hospital are closed.          _____

2   The dog is running on the wall behind the cat.          _____

3   The ambulance driver is pushing an old
    woman in her chair.          _____

4   The helicopter is orange and has got three
    stripes on it.          _____

5   The ambulance has got lights on the top at
    the back.          _____

6   A doctor is looking after a little boy with a
    broken leg.          _____

7   The two nurses who are talking are wearing
    pink uniforms.          _____

# Part 3

– 5 questions –

Emma is talking to her friend, Mary. What does Mary say?

Read the conversation and choose the best answer. Write a letter (A–H) for each answer.

You do not need to use all the letters. There is one example.

**Example**

> Emma: Hi Mary. Are you going to Sarah's party?
>
> Mary: _____ C

**Questions**

1 Emma: So what are you going to get her?

   Mary: _____

2 Emma: Don't you think that'll be too expensive?

   Mary: _____

3 Emma: I thought I'd get a game for her new computer.

   Mary: _____

4 Emma: Tomorrow after school, I think.

   Mary: _____

5 Emma: Yes, OK. I'll meet you in the hall after lessons.

   Mary: _____

A    That sounds good! Where are you going to get it?

B    Great and maybe I'll look for a cheaper present!

C    Yes, but I haven't got her present yet.          **(Example)**

D    Oh, that's a great idea! When are you going to get it?

E    Well, shall we go together then?

F    I don't know what present to get!

G    I'm not sure. I was thinking about a camera.

H    Oh, it might be. What are you getting her then?

# Part 4

**– 6 questions –**

**Read the story. Choose a word from the box. Write the correct word next to numbers 1–5. There is one example.**

Last year I was staying with my family in a __lovely__ hotel by the sea. From our window we could see a small island. And that's when Dad decided to get a boat! We took a picnic and a few blankets and then we were **(1)** _____ to the island. We weren't far from the island when it started to get windy and Dad hit a dangerous **(2)** _____ . That was the end of the boat!

We swam to the island, sat on the sand and ate our sandwiches. But then a storm came and it started to get **(3)** _____ so we went inside a cave. Dad had a **(4)** _____ with him so we could still see. He found somewhere dry and Mum put the blankets on the ground. And that's where we all slept for the night! The next day a big boat full of people **(5)** _____ on the island and our adventure was over!

| | | |
|---|---|---|
| **example** | | |
| lovely | torch | dark |
| visiting | arrived | sailing |
| rock | arriving | brave |

(6) **Now choose the best name for the story.**

**Tick one box.**

An interesting island ☐

An exciting adventure ☐

A terrible holiday ☐

# Part 5

**Look at the picture and read the story. Write some words to complete the sentences about the story. You can use 1, 2, 3 or 4 words.**

## At the bank

My name's Tony and I'm a photographer. I work for a big newspaper in the city. Yesterday morning I was going to a hotel in town to take some pictures of famous singers. I was walking past the bank and I suddenly decided to go in because I needed to get some money to buy lunch later.

But when I was inside I knew something was wrong. There was a man wearing a black sweater. I couldn't see his face but he was holding a big plastic bag. A woman was putting money into it. I knew then that he was stealing the money so I shouted 'Stop that right now!' He turned round and I took his picture. He was very surprised! He just dropped the money and then, before I could catch him, he ran out of the bank. Everyone said they thought I was very brave and they thanked me.

Then a policeman arrived and asked me lots of questions. Someone told him that I had a picture of the man. But the policeman asked, 'Why did you take his picture?' and said it was a dangerous thing to do. I felt stupid. Then the policeman took my camera away so I didn't get my photos of famous people that day!

## Examples

Tony works as a _____photographer_____.

Yesterday he had to go _____to a hotel_____ in town.

## Questions

1  Tony went into the bank because he wanted to
   _____ for lunch.

2  Tony _____ when he walked into the bank.

3  Tony saw a man who had _____ in his
   hands.

4  The man looked _____ when Tony took his
   picture.

5  Before he ran away, the man _____.

6  Everyone in the bank told Tony that he was
   _____.

7  The policeman took Tony's camera away so he couldn't take
   pictures of _____.

# Part 6

**Read the text. Choose the right words and write them on the lines.**

## The Sahara Desert

**Example**

The Sahara Desert is the _____biggest_____ of 22 deserts and is sometimes called the Sea of Sand. The temperature can be very high and there is very little

**1** water there _____ it doesn't rain very often.

An 'oasis' is like a lake in the desert. The water in an

**2** oasis comes from rivers _____ the ground. There are many 'oases' in the Sahara desert but

**3** people often _____ to travel for many days to find one.

Although life is difficult in the Sahara, a lot of

**4** people _____ live there. They move from one place to another to find the water they need

**5** and use camels to carry _____ when they move. Camels have large feet which means that they

**6** can walk easily _____ the rocks and sand.

**7** Lots of _____ animals and insects live in the Sahara too: snakes, lizards and spiders, for example.

**8** These animals get _____ of their water from

**9** the plants they eat. _____ the day small desert animals look for cool caves to sleep in and other animals lie down under trees. And did you

**10** _____ that the Sahara is growing every year?

| **Example** | big | bigger | biggest |
| --- | --- | --- | --- |
| I | but | because | then |
| 2 | under | between | into |
| 3 | has | have | had |
| 4 | still | also | yet |
| 5 | something | anything | everything |
| 6 | across | above | opposite |
| 7 | both | another | other |
| 8 | many | most | more |
| 9 | Until | During | Since |
| 10 | know | knew | known |

# Part 7

*– 5 questions –*

**Read the diary and write the missing words. Write one word on each line.**

**Example**

> Hello everyone!
>
> I'm __having__ a great time here with Michael.
> Yesterday we went to see a football match and I
> 1   was happy – my team _____ 5-3! It was
> very exciting! And I spoke to a friendly footballer
> 2   but I didn't know _____ he was!
> 3   Tomorrow we're _____ to go to the
> swimming pool. The swimming pool's outside but it
> 4   should be nice _____ the weather's good!
> 5   _____ you having a good time at home?
> I'm coming back on Thursday.
> See you then!
> Tom

# Speaking

## Find the Differences

## Information Exchange

### Candidate's copy

| Katy's Lesson | |
|---|---|
| Teacher | Mr Hall |
| What subject | Geography |
| How long | two hours |
| What day | Wednesday |
| What / study today | maps |

| Michael's Lesson | |
|---|---|
| Teacher | ? |
| What subject | ? |
| How long | ? |
| What day | ? |
| What / study today | ? |

### Examiner's copy

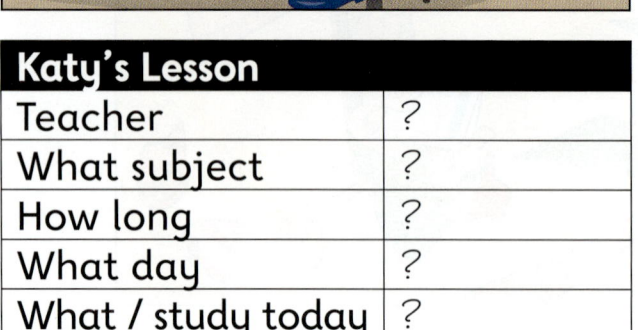

| Katy's Lesson | |
|---|---|
| Teacher | ? |
| What subject | ? |
| How long | ? |
| What day | ? |
| What / study today | ? |

| Michael's Lesson | |
|---|---|
| Teacher | Mrs Green |
| What subject | English |
| How long | one hour |
| What day | Tuesday |
| What / study today | spelling |

# Picture Story

# Flyers Vocabulary List

Students at this level are also expected to be familiar with all the words in the YLE Starters and Movers Vocabulary List which can be found in the Cambridge YLE Tests handbook.

**n** = noun
**v** = verb
**adj** = adjective
**prep** = preposition
**num** = number

**det** = determiner
**adv** = adverb
**conj** = conjunction
**pron** = pronoun
**int** = interrogative

**dis** = discourse marker
**int** = interjection
**excl** = exclamation
**poss** = possessive

## A

a.m. *for time*
across **prep**
actor **n**
after **adv + conj**
ago **adv**
agree **v**
air **n**
airport **n**
already **adv**
also **adv**
ambulance **n**
anyone **pron**
anything **pron**
anywhere **adv**
April **n**
arrive **v**
art **n**
artist **n**
astronaut **n**
August **n**
autumn **n**
away **adv**

## B

before **adv + conj**
begin **v**
believe **v**
belt **n**

bicycle **n**
bin **n**
biscuit **n** (US cookie)
bookshop **n**
bored **adj**
brave **adj**
break **v**
bridge **n**
broken **adj**
brush **n + v**
burn **v**
bus stop **n**
business **n**
businessman/woman **n**
butter **n**
butterfly **n**

## C

camel **n**
camp **v**
candy **n** (UK sweet(s))
card **n**
castle **n**
cave **n**
century **n**
cheap **adj**
chemist('s) **n**
chocolate **n**
chopsticks **n**
Christmas **n**

circus **n**
club **n**
college **n**
comb **n + v**
competition **n**
conversation **n**
cook **n**
cooker **n**
cookie **n** (UK biscuit)
corner **n**
could **v** (for possibility)
cut **v**

## D

dangerous **adj**
dark **adj**
date **n** (as in time)
dear **adj** (as in Dear Harry)
December **n**
decide **v**
dentist **n**
desert **n**
diary **n**
dictionary **n**
dinousaur **n**
drum **n**
dry **adj**
during **prep**

## E

each **det + pron**
early **adj + adv**
east **n**
else **adv**
empty **adj**
end **v**
engineer **n**
enough **adj + pron**
envelope **n**
environment **n**
ever **adv**
everyone **pron**
everything **pron**
everywhere **adv**
exam **n**
excellent **adj + excl**
excited **adj**
expensive **adj**
explain **v**
extinct **adj**

## F

factory **n**
fall **v**
fall over **v**
far **adj + adv**
fast **adj + adv**
February **n**
feel **v**
fetch **v**
a few **det**
find out **v**
finish **v**
fire **n**
fire engine **n**
fireman/woman **n**
fire station **n**
flag **n**
flashlight **n** (UK torch)
flour **n**

fog **n**
foggy **adj**
follow **v**
footballer **n**
for **prep of time**
forget **v**
fork **n**
fridge **n**
friendly **adj**
front **adj + n**
full **adj**
fun **adj + n**
fur **n**
future **n**

## G

geography **n**
get off **v**
get on **v**
get to **v**
glass **adj**
glove **n**
glue **n + v**
go out **v**
gold **adj + n**
golf **n**
group **n**
grow **v**
guess **n + v**

## H

half **adj + n**
happen **v**
hard **adj + adv**
hate **v**
hear **v**
heavy **adj**
high **adj**
hill **n**
history **n**
horrible **adj**

hotel **n**
hour **n**
husband **n**

## I

ice **n**
if **conj**
ill **adj**
important **adj**
insect **n**
interesting **adj**
into **prep**

## J

jam **n**
January **n**
job **n**
journalist **n**
July **n**
June **n**
just **adv**

## K

key **n**
kilometre **n** (US kilometer)
kind **adj**
knife **n**

## L

language **n**
late **adj + adv**
later **adv**
leave **v**
left **adj + n** (as in direction)
let **v**
letter **n** (as in mail)
lie **v** (as in lie down)
light **adj + n**
little **adj**

a little **adv + det**
London **n**
look after **v**
look like **v**
lovely **adj**
low **adj**

## M

magazine **n**
March **n**
married **adj**
maths **n** (US math)
May **n** (as in month)
may **v**
meal **n**
mechanic **n**
medicine **n**
meet **v**
meeting **n**
metal **adj + n**
midday **n**
midnight **n**
might **v**
mind **v**
minute **n**
missing **adj**
mix **v**
money **n**
month **n**
much **adv + det + pron**
museum **n**

## N

news **n**
newspaper **n**
next **adj + adv**
noisy **adj**
no-one **pron**
north **n**
November **n**
nowhere **adv**

## O

o'clock **adv**
October **n**
octopus **n**
of course **adv**
office **n**
once **adv**
other **det + pron**
over **adv + prep**

## P

p.m. *for time*
painter **n**
paper **adj + n**
past **n + prep**
pepper **n**
perhaps **adv**
photographer **n**
piece **n**
pilot **n**
pizza **n**
planet **n**
plastic **adj + n**
plate **n**
player **n**
pocket **n**
policeman/woman **n**
police station **n**
poor **adj**
post **v**
postcard **n**
post office **n**
prefer **v**
problem **n**
programme **n** (US program)
pull **v**
push **v**
pyramid **v**

## Q

quarter **n**
queen **n**

## R

race **n + v**
ready **adj**
remember **v**
restaurant **n**
rich **adj**
right **adj + n** (as in direction)
ring **n**
rocket **n**
rucksack **n**

## S

salt **n**
same **adj**
science **n**
scissors **n**
score **n + v**
secret **n**
secretary **n**
sell **v**
send **v**
September **n**
shelf **n**
shorts **n**
should **v**
silver **adj + n**
since **prep**
singer **n**
single **adj**
ski **n + v**
sky **n**
sledge **n + v**
smell **n + v**
snack **n**
snowball **n**
snowman **n**

so **adv + conj**
soap **n**
soft **adj**
someone **pron**
somewhere **adv**
soon **adv**
sound **n + v**
south **n**
space **n**
speak **v**
spend **v**
spoon **n**
spot **n**
spotted **adj**
spring **n**
stamp **n**
station **n**
stay **v**
steal **v**
still **adv**
storm **n**
straight on **adv**
strange **adj**
stripe **n**
striped **adj**
student **n**
study **v**
subject **n**
suddenly **adv**
sugar **n**
suitcase **n**
summer **n**
sure **adj**
surname **n**
swan **n**
sweet(s) **n** (US candy)
swing **n + v**

# T

take **v** (as in time e.g. it takes 20 minutes)
tape recorder **n**

taste **n + v**
taxi **n**
teach **v**
team **n**
telephone **n**
tent **n**
thank **v**
theatre **n**
through **prep**
tidy **adj + v**
tights **n**
time **n**
together **adv**
toilet **n**
tomorrow **adv + n**
tonight **adv + n**
torch **n** (US flashlight)
traffic **n**
turn **v**
turn off **v**
turn on **v**
twice **adv**

# U

umbrella **n**
unfriendly **adj**
unhappy **adj**
uniform **n**
university **n**
untidy **adj**
until **prep**
use **v**
usually **adv**

# V

visit **v**
volleyball **n**

# W

waiter **n**
warm **adj**

way **n**
west **n**
where **pron**
whisper **v**
whistle **v**
wife **n**
will **v**
William **n**
win **v**
wing **n**
winter **n**
wish **n + v**
without **prep**
wood **n**
wool **n**

# X

(no words at this level)

# Y

year **n**
yet **adv**

# Z

zero **n**